HOW YOU CAN BECOME A
SUCCESSFUL
ENTREPRENEUR!

Introducing:
THE BUSINESS BOOT CAMP

REGINALD T. HARDAWAY, Sr., MS, Ed.D

WESTBOW
PRESS®
A DIVISION OF THOMAS NELSON
& ZONDERVAN

WestBow Press books may be ordered through booksellers or by contacting:

WestBow Press
A Division of Thomas Nelson & Zondervan
1663 Liberty Drive
Bloomington, IN 47403
www.westbowpress.com
844-714-3454

ISBN: 978-1-6642-0632-8 (sc)
ISBN: 978-1-6642-0633-5 (hc)
ISBN: 978-1-6642-0631-1 (e)

Library of Congress Control Number: 2020918409

Print information available on the last page.

WestBow Press rev. date: 10/14/2020

CONTENTS

INTRODUCTION

If you have the desire to start your own business, this is the book for you. It will not only help you get started but will also help you create and maintaining the structure of the business.

You will learn how to incorporate your business, establish the financial reports, and other necessary information. It will even tell you how to succeed from the business if one day, you decide to sell and retire.

I was researching the newspapers, and in an article, the author stated that AMERICA WAS LAST IN BUSINESS START-UPS. I thought to myself, how could that be? I had taught business at the college level for nearly two decades, most of those years were in the MBA programs, and I knew I had to do something to assist future entrepreneurs. Therefore, I decided to write this book.

In this book, you will discover everything from incorporating your business, to creating a balance sheet, income statement, and growing your business. America, we need to grow more businesses and create jobs and opportunities for our people. When God gives you a gift, share it with others.

CHAPTER 1

Theory X Manager Style

In a manuscript entitled AN ALPHABET CUISINE FOR MANAGERS: Theories X, Y & Z, I discussed how I have viewed employers throughout the country.

Ladies and gentlemen, it is show time, and now I introduce to you the star of our show, Theory X Drill Sergeant of management. Yes, the Drill Sergeant of Management is what the Theory X Manager is. The Theory X style management tells you what to do, how to do it, and how long it should take you to complete the assignment. The employee gives little if any input. You better not ask questions and had better be on time with the assignment. Theory X managers are, perhaps, a modern form of mental slavery.

In the Executive (1981) Harry Levison discussed Doug McGregor, the father of Theory X, Theory Y Management. He stated that McGregor discussed the importance of good leadership and how it is essentially dependent on the manager's concept of what his job is and what management is. This analysis by McGregor may have a ring of truth to it. Good management does not only depend on what the manager believes his job is and what management is, but it also dependents on the manager's social and economic background. What does this manager bring to the table from his/her upbringing? A manager who truly has a Christian perspective may be uncertain about taking part in a sting to sabotage another individual in the workplace, whereas a manager who does not have a conscious may not be disturbed by this undertaking.

Managers also bring their academic training to the management table, but they also bring their early views of life instilled by their parents. This does not mean an individual cannot rise above a negative, sexist or racist upbringing. It does mean that they need to have the will and desire to do so. McGregor believes that good management also depends on personal convictions and beliefs about people.

Levinson further believes that the "personality" of an organization reflects its founding fathers. He says the founder or head sets a standard of behavior and a kind of structure. I believe this behavior and structure manifest into a culture a corporate culture. This is perhaps, what the west-coast health-maintenance organization was all about.

THIS RETAILER WENT FROM FIRST TO LAST

After a tour of duty in the healthcare field, I went to work for the world's largest retailer. It did not take long for me to discover that their corporate culture was not fair and perhaps primitive. The Theory X managers excelled at being mean and low-down to people of color, females and foreigners. That fall, I entered their accelerated checklist, master's program. The program was a fast-track program that was, perhaps, used to produce the federal statistics needed to satisfy their equal opportunity public lie. The rotation was excellent, and much was learned.

I was later assigned to the Buying Dept for Floor Covering. After completing a successful tour in the Floor Dept, I was transferred to the company's furniture-buying department. The big -ticket department had one African American checklist male, Chuck, who was serving in the Assistant Buying position on table accessories. Furniture was possibly the biggest moneymaking department in the company. The National Manager, Senior Buyers, Buyers and Marketing Manager made big bucks.

The culture shifted abruptly when I became a full-time regular employee. In the furniture buying department, my first assignment in marketing was the ORANGE BOOK. The furniture buying department with the cooperation of the other home furnishing departments, i.e. floor covering and bedding, issued the ORANGE BOOK with an orange binder to the 800 stores throughout the country. It displayed different room scenes of living rooms, dining rooms, bedrooms and family rooms with stock numbers, buying and selling prices, and other relevant vendor information that only the different departments would know. These rooms were to be duplicated in the 800 stores, and the book offered buying information for everything in the picture from the figurine on the table to the rug on the floor. I felt this was an excellent concept.

Our laboratory was a square block facility in Chicago's west side not far from the Sears Tower. As the marketing representative for this project, I was responsible for setting up the different scenes and accessorizing them with the help of a Stylist. Diana, the previous organizer, had received total cooperation from everybody in the Home Furniture Department. She also had the staff to physically move the furniture into the various room scenes for photographing before the Stylist accessorized it with lamps, figurines bedspreads, greenery etc. When I stepped into the same role Diane had, buyers began to drag their feet.

They delayed when it came to supply the same moving support. Suddenly, they wanted me to lift the furniture into the room scenes. This had never been done before. They even dragged their feet when it came to finalize the contract with the photography studio who completed the color separations. It was obvious to me what was happening. They wanted me to fail. When I confronted the Marketing Manager and National Manager with this information, their response was "Reggie you have to get them to work with you". Make them work with me? This is a corporate project. Why do I have to make them work with me?

In true Theory Management style, they offered little support. I felt them had agreed not to support me in this project. When I mentioned Diane had not had this level of difficulty and that I had a hernia repair a few years ago, it did not faze them. They reverted to the slave master mentality of the slave being lazy. Finally, they agreed to hire three young African American men to assist in setting up the room scenes. A photographer was on board and the studio was also on board to complete the project. We lost precious time during these foolish games, but that is what Theory X managers do. However, in this case, it was tainted with a heavy dose of America's racism.

The photography studio assigned somebody to work with me and aid in completing the project. Diane, who had moved to another assignment, the Stylist Jim, Geno, the lab maintenance person and I were leaving the lab on Chicago's west side after working all day on setting up the room scenes. Jim, Geno and I waited downstairs for the bus to take us back to the Sears Tower. Diane came down her face was beet red and stated she had stopped to use the restroom and were left upstairs with those "spooks". She stopped in the middle of her sentence, realizing that I was in the mix. After reporting the incident to human resources, the human resource director just knew Fred, the National Manager, had dealt with the situation. I told him that, not only did he not deal with it, but the Marketing Manager did not deal with it neither and it was totally acceptable to these people. Every time you hear of this company doing badly, remember God said, "Touch not my anointed". To date, the company that was making $20 billion a year has gone under.

CHAPTER II

Theory Y Management Style

Theory Y style of management unlike Theory X, is more employee friendly and humane. It empowers, respects, includes, celebrates and encourages. It feels good to the person being celebrated as well as to those employees who are observing the celebration. Remember, psychologists say that when you contribute to someone feeling good, those who observe the incident also feel good.

Amazingly, Theory Y management is not widely celebrated in the United States. I had a difficult time coming up with American corporations who practice this style of management. Some believe it goes against the American grain, culture, and disposition. After all, John Wayne was not a Theory Y kind of guy.

There are a few American corporations that have little, if any, job turnover because people refuse to leave dye to quality Theory Y management styles. They are few and far between, but some do exist. The love of company may be a byproduct of the respect and inclusion shared in the workplace. Progressive managers, teachers, and leaders move their people toward Theory Y style of management a management of empowerment, respect and trust. Besides, it feels good to the employee and employer and it creates a friendlier atmosphere in the workplace.

William Glasser, MD in his Quality School (1989) and Hardaway, Ed. D (1998) proved through relevant research that quality is possible in the workplace and classroom. The research showed that schools and corporations are not that different when it comes to getting people to unite and work together. Both the schools and corporations are managing people who want their needs met. Corporations, unlike schools, can fire insubordinate employees, but the needs are the same for the student and corporate employee. The student and employee say respect me and include me in the planning process. Yes, include your students in the planning process.

WHAT IS LEAD MANAGEMENT?

Lead management is a management style that is centered on leading rather than telling. Leader managers organize and brainstorm with teams to discuss solutions to corporate problems and future products. Leader management compared to boss management, Theory X, gets better results. Employees and students ae more involved in the planning and implementation process. The atmosphere is much more pleasant, and the absenteeism is minimal.

Lead-management employers view their employees as an asset and not a liability. The line item is not on the corporate balance sheet; however, employees are as much an asset as office equipment or patents. For example, on a corporate trip to the twin cities and the 3M Corporation, I learned that 3M, with its open creative policy, had employees returning to work on their off days to assist with innovative projects. That is how the stick-up product was created. In comparison, teachers who utilize lead-management style of managing have joy restored to the lives of the students. Research has shown that scores increase, and bad behavior decrease when lead-management is implemented.

WHAT IS EMPOWERMENT

Empowerment is giving an employee or student the authority to perform quality work with confidence and flexibility. Empowerment believes in an employee's ability to get the job done in an efficient, quality and timely fashion. Managers who use the empowerment method are called Theory Y managers. They possess confidence in their ability to hire qualified, competent individuals and then they permit them to take off.

They take off after receiving proper training and having brainstorming and planning sections with their managers who allow them to implement the company's strategy. Empowerment is not an unorganized, sporadic venture, quite the contrary, it is a well-planned venture that is field tested and implemented with "total quality" and a "world-class" plan. Unlike the early industrial periods in American history, "total quality" refers to performing everything with total quality as the goal. Everything from raw materials, goods in process, and the finished goods are pushed through the process with quality in mind. The successful companies perform to the plan put forth by senior management with input from other individuals in the company. These are the successful entities; those which fail, like many persons discussed in Chapter 1, are often individually motivated and often drive the corporate bus into the lake.

WHY DO EMPLOYEES FAIL TO USE QUALITY?

Many people use only what they know, and what they do not know can fill a house. There are managers who have never heard of Theories X, Y, Z or lead management. They were trained to tell the employee what to do and how to do it, like a parent. Many were also trained to disrespect the employee, with no regard for their personhood. The employees, prior to Theory Y, had little if any corporate input. Some years later, there came a paradigm shift, which is partly what we know today.

Also, there are corporations which fail to give sufficient training to their managers on how to manage and relate to their "subordinates" whatever that is! After all, the United States has a culture of slavery and inhumanity. Many corporations are so focused on the dollar bill that they fail to realize the needs of their customers, who bring in the dollar bills they so deeply love. In other words, treat your employees and customers right and the money will flow. They are "frozen in time" and fail to see the big picture.

This was the attitude of people like Frederick Taylor from yester-year. We are now learning that culture training has a great deal to do with how people respect and supervise others.

What happens when the corporate culture is established on quicksand? Well, like a house built on quicksand or the wolf who wanted to bow the house down, it results in disaster. For years, some American businesses preached "no Blacks or Jews, eliminating Blacks and Jews from the workforce. In the case of Jews, they had the foresight to create their own. They did not wait for someone to employ them; they bought the business. How brilliant! Many businesses also closed the door on the opportunity to bring the females and other people who may have kept them afloat and increased their ability to blacken their bottom line. Foolishly, they limited and robbed themselves and society of competent and qualified workers based on lies and deceit from yester-year.

Some of these companies are no longer in business, and I, for one, do not miss them. They closed their doors within three years or less or survived a century and the truth caught up with them. I believe it was Dr. King who said in his I HAVE A DREAM speech (1993) that truth pressed against the earth shall raise again. Respecting others has merit.

DIVERSITY IN THE WORKPLACE

Diversity has almost come to the workplace. The past saw quite a few Caucasian males occupy the top seats in corporations. They made the big money and got the promotions, many times because of who they were, although nobody would admit it. Today, some minority individuals and women are taking the workplace into the 21st century. I believe mostly females. Because we now live in a global economy, skills will matter more than race and gender. The proof of this phenomenon is the internet. Entrepreneurs are making thousands of dollars becoming internet entrepreneurs. I often wonder if the invention of the compute was God's way of leveling the playing field. Historically, according to the late Dr. Barbara Sizemore, a former elementary teacher at Chicago's Shoop Elementary School and my alma mater, who later became the Superintendent of Schools for Washington, DC, White males, followed by Black males were the money makers; Black women were at the bottom of the totem pole. This might have been true in the 60s, but as we enter the 21st Century, many Black men have systematically been eliminated from the workforce, including some Ph.Ds.

SOME THEORY Y PEOPLE

Some Theory Y people I have encountered. Starting with sports, Jerry Manuel, former Chicago White Sox manager, has made me proud. I never thought I would see an African American manager on the southside of Chicago. During my childhood, when Blacks were not allowed to be Andy Frain ushers at the baseball stadiums, I never thought I would see such an event. I wanted so badly to be an Andy Frain usher. As an adult, I had the pleasure of attending the same church with Mr. Manuel and his family. He had the Theory Y style of management, although, a few times, he had to share his feelings with the umpires throughout the league. I felt some of that was just show for the players and fans. Although some fans saw him as passive, Jerry was anything but passive. He walked and managed in faith.

John Cunea, my high school Latin teacher at Chicago's Morgan Park High School, was a Theory Y individual. I loved his class. Although my Latin was not the best, he made his students feel valued. Theory Y people make people feel valued. Before class, Mr. Cunea would often greet us at the door with a huge smile. He had white hair, pearly white teeth, and wore a white-on-white shirt and blue suit. He guided us, with love and respect, taught Latin with ease and made his classes enjoyable. I thank God for Mr. Cunea! Who made his transition a few years ago.

Today, I use some of his techniques with my graduate students. I am caring and understanding when I help solve a school issue. As life would have it, I was blessed to meet Mr. Cunea's niece a few years ago. After being referred to me by Dr. Pamela Hardaway, my cousin, I met his niece in a McDonald's restaurant in Tinley Park, Illinois. She was interested in Dr. William Glasser's and the quality school concept and Pam referred her to me. After completing our formal discussion, we engaged in some small talk and I discovered that she was Mr. Cunea's niece I had to fight back tears! I sent him my love and I learned shortly after this visit that he left us.

After high school, I held a part-time position at Chicago's Marshall Field retail store in downtown Chicago. I worked the store on State and Randolph in the heart of Chicago's Loop. This was a great opportunity for people who wanted to work part-time while attending college.

The supervisors were kind and the hours were flexible. Every year, they hired summer and Christmas help and Christmas at Marshall Field was unique and wonderful. I was most impressed with their corporate culture. They believed in quality in every area of their stores and satisfying the customer at all costs. I was blessed to meet employees who had worked at Fields for thirty and forty years. The only bad thing they reported was the pay. Field did not pay well, but it gave the employees a level of security.

Some of the supervisors at Fields practiced Theory Y style of management. Mr. Eck, Mr. Cwik, and their senior manager Mr. Davis, who was as cool as singer Jerry Butler the "ice man". Marshall Field perpetuated a professional and pleasant atmosphere that was second to none. One of the managers, Mr. Ryan, a short blonde Caucasian gentleman who stood 5'5" was my manager in the Shop 57. Shop 57 was a unique area that housed dresses in the thousands of dollars. Mr. Ryan was kind and never said much unless it was job related. He would always add "thanks" to everything he would ask the employees to do. He was a fantastic gentleman and I often think of these people today. In the 60s, when America was racially and socially divided, they showed me the utmost of respect.

The 3M Corporation is another Theory Y company which shows the utmost of respect to its employees. While working in retail for Sears, I took a business trip to the 3M headquarters in Minnesota. The company sent a 10-passenger Lear Jet to pick us up at Meigs Field in Chicago's Loop. The experience was simply wonderful. We landed and toured the facility, seeking their business as an alternative to Scotchgard. Scotchgard is a fabric protector that is applied to floor covering and bedding. Sears wanted to get a piece of the market, and the national manager and senior buyers decided to approach 3M Corporation.

What impressed me the most was the attitude of their employees. Rumor had it that employees are so enthusiastic that many came in on their days off to assist with innovative projects. The results are evident in the way they crated new and fresh ideas for their customers. During the trip, I was told that the Post-it note pad was created by these wonderful employees. Completing my doctorate degree at the University of Sarasota, I saw excellence in the way Drs. John Delp and Peter Simmons went about their work. They were gregarious and had professional and enjoyable classrooms that showed value to their students. Both gentlemen were successful in their private practices and saw teaching as something they enjoyed on the side. Perhaps a calling on their lives! Today, in my classroom situations, I use the same caring and professional practices that were taught by these wonderful individuals. Thank you!

ROCKWELL INTERNATIONAL CORPORATION – SEIZE-THE MOMENT

Rockwell International Corporation, like a good Y company, remembered its employees. Their strategic plan was to upgrade the manufacturing and engineering departments. The plan called for promoting the information technology program as a total part of the company's strategic plan and not an independent department plan. Their challenge ranged from automotive to aerospace-production parts. They knew if they were going to compete on a global basis, they had to face the challenge of a global information system.

Technology had played a major role in helping Rockwell International Corporation build a network in Europe and the Far East. The example of Rockwell being involved in the automobile business was their ability to deliver a sunroof to Volkswagen in just 136 minutes after receiving the order. They were aware of having the proper technology in place at the correct time.

With technology changing every minute, the challenge to Rockwell was to stay abreast of new and innovative ideas to better serve their customers. They streamlined their manufacturing process to eliminate unnecessary handling. The scenario seen by Rockwell pulling its raw materials into process when the time was appropriate and the ability to access the history regarding the sunroof cars enabled them to ship in less than 3 hours.

Rockwell International corporation employed over seventy-thousand employees and had annual sales of nearly $12 million at that time. They were not a new kid on the block. They are over 80 years old with many subsidies. Love it!

CHASE MANHATTAN BANK

Courage played a major role in the success of Chase Manhattan Bank. They were committed to Microsoft Windows even when it was not popular to do so. In 1990, when Case took this giant step, it was a risky business move for the multibillion-dollar corporation. But they were determined to simplify the technology process and Microsoft was the choice. "Our change" said their information Chief Craig Goldman, "as we go into the future, is to simplify the presentation and provide the ease of one interface to all uses". The information-system staff turned to a variety of Windows software to help in this venture, but they chose Easel Visual Basic and Excel spreadsheet. They also chose Pilot Executive software, Lotus Notes and 1-2-3 for Windows for electronic mail, working grouping computing and spreadsheets from Lotus Development Corporation. Chase Manhattan Bank (USA) are in Wilmington, Delaware, and has over twenty-five hundred employees and showed annual sales of over $10 billion.

EMPLOYER SHARES MILLIONS

Some years ago, the Chicago Tribune printed an article entitled "Man Sells Multimillion Dollar firm, Shares Wealth with 550 Workers". I thought to myself that this is totally unheard of! Bob Thompson sold Thompson-McCully Co. in Belleville, Michigan for $442 million and shared some of the proceeds with his 550 employees. The article stated that Bob Thompson had shared a vision with his wife and a few other individuals to sell and decided to follow through. He later issued a letter to his employees stating that upon selling they would not lose their jobs but would share in the proceeds of the sale. How about it! Mr. Thompson divided $128 million among 550 employees. He also gave more than 80 a case bonus, making them millionaires. Pastor Charles Stanley of Atlanta, in a Sunday-morning sermon, also mentioned Mr. Thompson. He said, "a part of our blessings in the next life would be the good we do in this life".

CHAPTER III

Theory Z, The Japanese Mangement Style

Keen competition exists in Japan for school age children to perform well. To perform well in school equates to a lifetime job in one of Japan's total quality industries.

There are those who believe the Theory Z concept began prior to William Ouchi. It is believed that when Edward Deming, Ph. D decided to move to Japan after World War II and introduce the Japanese to the total quality concept, it may have been the beginning of the process. Dr. Deming was disrespected and denied his total-quality ideas in his home country of America and, like Christ, took it elsewhere. Being denied the use of total quality in the American automobile industry, he decided to take it across the waters to Japan.

The Japanese and their automobile industry received him with open arms and the rest is history as the impact the Japanese have made on the automobile industry. As a matter of fact, prior to this writing, the American automobile industry has asked and were granted under President Barak Obama billions of dollars to save the industry. A lack of quality across the board was one of the biggest complaints.

Years after Deming's departure, William Ouchi discussed his Theory Z style of management. Theory Z was perhaps seen as more empowering than Theory Y and Theory X. He touched on three managerial assumptions to prove his point. He discussed workers' motivation, workers' attitude toward work, and what works for employees. The Theory Z manager, according to Dr. Braden, assumes that employees are motivated by a strong sense of commitment to be a part of something worthwhile. Of course, the Theory X manager assumes the worker is motivated by money and the Theory Y manager assumes that the employees are motivated by their needs to fulfill their social esteem, self-actualization, and security.

Professor Braden further believes that when it comes to workers' attitudes toward work, that the Theory Z manager believes that employees will not only seek out opportunities for responsibility, but they crave the opportunity to advance and learn more about their employer. This is diametrical to the Theory X manager, who assumes that the employees dislike work, avoids responsibility, and work for the two big monthly pay periods. Could he be projecting his own feelings? However, the Theory Y manger is a little better, as he/she believes that employees see work as a natural activity and will seek out opportunities to have increased responsibilities and become more of a team player.

When the question is raised, "What will work with employees? The Theory Z manager, again, leads the way, followed by the Theory Y manager. The Theory Z manager believes employees should learn the business through the various departments, coming up through the ranks slowly, and that the best way benefits will be obtained. The Theory X manager believes that workers will only respond to coercion, control and directions, or threats of punishment or firing. Again, Theory Y comes in second when it says workers will respond best to favorable working conditions that do not pose threats or strong control.

▌ IS AMERICAN A THEORY Z NATION?

Few individuals believe that America has what it takes to become a Theory Z nation. Others wonder, with the focus on the corporate bottom line and little focus on the employees, how could they obtain this higher level of managerial excellence. Afterall, Americans are more concerned about the bottom line and other unimportant events.

American corporations had their opportunity with Edward Deming, MD and rejected him and his total quality concept. Michael Gerber explained quite eloquently with his E-Myth philosophy, that an entrepreneur must work "on" the business, before working "in" the business. Ray Kroc may have perfected this concept as he built McDonald's Corporation into a money empire and Mr. Watson when he performed the same miracle with IBM.

Many believe, and I am one of those, that America can never become a Theory Z corporation because of its lack of humanity and love of money. First, American corporations focus too much on their bottom line and have little corporate balance throughout their corporate systems. They fail to recognize that it is the needs of the customer and fulfilling those needs that answers the question about the bottom line. Secondly, it is impossible to be a Theory Z corporation if you fail to practice humanity. Too many are fond of sexism and racism. American corporations invest time and money telling everyone how they are an "equal opportunity employer" and not enough time becoming one. Most people know this is government enforced and not corporately desired. Thirdly, for decades American corporations have failed to pay women and minorities equal pay for an equal day's work. This speaks volumes about American corporations and America. When an individual is forced to 'do the right thing' what does that say about a society which claims to be the best? For years, it was believed that just as a lack of quality has caught up with American automobile corporations, which other manufacturers are waiting in line for the same results? As the Beatles sing: When will they ever learn?

CHAPTER IV

Information for Entrepreneurs

Develop the structure of your business before working in your business. Often, individuals become so anxious to turn the key that they fail to put a structure in place for the business. Your structure should include everything from how the telephone calls will be answered to employees dressing for success.

Whatever structure being used, you should understand that deviating from that structure will lead to disciplinary action including dismissal. The structure you choose is that serious.

CREATING A BUSINESS PLAN

Although the Executive Summary is the initial topic in a Business Plan, it may be completed last. It is imperative to respect those reading the plan. In your Executive Summary, remember to include the meat of the plan. It is important because many bankers only read the Executive Summary portion of the Business Plan due to their busy schedules. To the point, state what you want them to know clearly and to the point.

CREATE A 5-YEAR EXCEL BUDGET

Using the Excel software, create a five-year projected budget for your business. This budget should include job titles, salaries, expenses, employee benefits, charitable contributions, and projected tax liabilities for up to five years. After the completion of the budget, then focus on preparing a Strategic Plan.

CREATING A STRATEGIC PLAN

Your Strategic Plan should clearly state where you are, where you want to go, and how you plan to get there. Included in your plan should be the research of experts in the industry, as well as, your own input.

Remember, when at the end of your plan, and evaluation is occurring, remember to re-evaluate. Do not hesitate to make changes, if necessary, as the industry is changing; and it will go through some changes. Finally, do not hesitate to invite other managers etc. into the planning process. Remember, in creating your business, there is a need to establish an atmosphere of Total Quality!

CREATING AN ATMOSPHERE OF TOTAL QUALITY

While developing your business structure, it is imperative that the company has a style of management that is productive and respectful. During the management training process, it should be emphasized that managing with coercion is not our goal. If one manages using coercion, the wrong manager has been hired. The managerial style of coercion, or Theory X style of management, breaks the employees down and leaves them feeling worthless and disrespected, and will eventually cause them to leave the company.

In creating an atmosphere of Total Quality, the workplace should be clean, mentally, physically and socially supportive.

THEORY Y, A STYLE OF MANAGEMENT THAT EMPOWERS

The company should include a style of management that creates quality for the newly formed company in every way possible. During managerial training, it should emphasize that respect and empowerment is a must for the success of the business. Managing using empowerment lifts and encourages employees to do their best. Additionally, creating a family spirit and motto will benefit the company in a positive and progressive way.

CREATING A BUSINESS MOTTO

Many businesspeople may tell you to OWN NOTHING BUT CONTROL EVERYTHING. Your newly created Business Trust will own your business assets, you are the Trustee, who will control the business. There are too many parasites who want something for nothing for the business not to be protected.

CREATE A HEALTHY WORKFORCE

While providing quality health insurance for your employees, also emphasize the importance of good health and reward those who have a healthy lifestyle like maintaining a healthy body weight and a non-smoking lifestyle. Have the employee's physician determine what a healthy body weight is allowing the employees to choose to participate.

CREATE A PROFESSIONAL DRESS CODE

The workplace is not the "go-go club". Other than working in the warehouse, the company should have a dress code that reflects dressing for success. Many believe that jeans and party attire are not appropriate for a professional business environment, and in many situations, I agree. The dress code should include input from the employees and should be a part of the corporate policies and reinforced during training.

REPRESENT WHAT IS GOOD & JUST

Your corporate culture should represent what is good and just. While negotiating with vendors, represent a win-win, mutual respect attitude, and allow both parties to leave with their dignity and respect intact.

Having a win-win attitude may develop a long-lasting relationship that will pay off in the short and long run.

Remember to always maintain a level head. You should not think more highly of yourself than you are.

KEEPING A LEVEL HEAD

There is a difficult climb up the ladder, but an abrupt decline on the way down. Speaking to the janitor as well as the executives is a healthy sign of respect for everybody in your organization. Making everybody feel appreciated and welcome in the organization should be your goal.

WELCOME DIVERSITY

Not only is diversity the law, but it is an asset for your organization. To hire good competent people should be your goal. Employees should know, without a doubt, that discrimination and racist attitudes are not acceptable.

SIGN YOUR OWN CHECKS

Under no circumstance are you to allow anybody in the company to sign your name on a check. This does not pertain to a $50 to $100 petty cash account, but when it comes to everything else, you should be aware of the disbursement, the purpose for the disbursement and your signature should be necessary to approve it. Do not be so busy to allow another to sign your checks. Never!!!

KNOW YOUR INDUSTRY

Remain abreast of your industry, and possible changes. Never hesitate to adjust your strategic plan when the industry is going in a different direction. Remember, in evaluating, there will be times when you need to evaluate and re-evaluate changes to your strategic plan and your budget.

Many times, this is necessary. Using the clock for example, there are some industries that make changes in the morning at 8:00 am, others may make changes at the noon hour. Your organization should never be the last or nearly last to make changes after everybody else has made their changes.

| USE NON-DISCLOSURES IN YOUR BUSINESS

Individuals whom you share intimate corporate information should sign a non-disclosure statement prior to receiving the information. This goes for employees, upon hiring, and non-employees when made aware of important corporate information.

It should be clear, upon hiring, that the sharing of information with any outside individual who is out of the loop, is a no-no and could lead to immediate dismissal and legal actions.

| CREATE A BUSINESS TRUST

Your business trust should own the assets of your business. Your family trust should own your personal assets. The two are separate and should remain that way. However, it is possible to lease your business assets from your family trust. Some individuals believe this trust should be Federal Trust. Speak to your attorney for further information.

| INVEST IN TANGIBLE ASSETS

Many believe the wealthy invest in tangible assets and view the Federal Reserve Note as a debt instrument that depreciates in value. Tangible assets like precious metals, land, collectible paintings etc. Appreciates in value. The Silver and Gold Eagle coins created in 1985 are legal tender and will make a great investment.

While teaching elementary school, I introduced my 8th grade class to silver when I purchased a ten-ounce bar for less than a hundred dollars in 1984 or 1985 and the students purchased a one once bar for less than $10. When I sold my ten- ounce bar around 2010, I was offered around $400.

▌ KNOW YOUR LOCAL LEADERS

Know your local political leaders, and if possible, introduce yourself to them. You may want to contribute to some of their campaigns and get to know some of the other entrepreneurs in the area. Both could become an asset to your organization.

▌ APPRECIATE & RESPECT YOUR EMPLOYEES

When possible bless your employees with bonuses. This bonus should be given to both salaried and non-salaried employees. Everybody!

Over train your managers. It is better to over train than under train them. Like an excellent baseball team that has an A+ minor league system, it pays off. You can never train too much!

If possible, create a scholarship program for your employees and their families. Investing in education of your employees and their children is wise and will be highly appreciated. If the children cannot be included, at least a scholarship for employees would be wonderful.

If possible, create an internship program for students in the community. Using the high schools in the community, create a program for juniors and or seniors to receive specialized training under your tutorage.

Finally, have an annual family picnic inviting the employees and their families to come out for a great time of celebration. You may also want to include tours of the facility.

▌ CREATE AN (IN) TRAPRENEUR PROGRAM

An intrapreneur program allowing inventions while working on their time in your facility allows them to share financially in those profits. 3M Corporation has such a program and have included the inventions by their employees in their line of products.

CHAPTER IV

Developing a Business Plan

Determine if your business will be incorporated in your home state or the state of Delaware. You may also decide to own and fund your business through a Federal Business Trust Fund. Some have reported this is important because, according to them, if sued, your business cannot be brought into local or state court, but in Federal Court only.

EXECUTIVE SUMMARY

The Executive Summary is extremely important. Because of the limited time many bankers have, they may only read the Executive Summary portion of the business plan. Therefore, beef it up and put relevant information in it. Some individuals choose to prepare it last after completing the other portions of the business plan.

The Executive Summary should include an Introduction to your plan. Prior to writing the Executive Summary, a Mission and Vision Statement should be written to include in this portion of the plan.

The Mission Statement should be a paragraph written in PRESENT TENSE that describes the intent of the business. For example: The XYZ Group is a management company designed to teach management and financial skills to businesses across the world in the form of seminars.

The Vision Statement should be a paragraph written in FUTURE TENSE that describes your future business plans. For example: The XYZ Group will become the number one global management company in the world.

Now that we have compiled the Mission Statement and Vision Statement, this information should be posted throughout the business to make the employees aware of your intent. We are now ready to compile the Introduction portion of your plan.

In the Introduction, you want to state:

- Name of Business
- Discuss the officers and their education & experience
- The kind of business owned: sole proprietorship, partnership or corporation
- Location of business, city, state, country etc.
- Funding of your business; amount of funds needed and if you are shovel ready
- The dimensions of the structure, if you are building a new structure or rehabbing and existing structure.
- Products & Services being offered
- Progress of business to date
- Demographics
- Mission Statement
- Vision Statement
- Present a SWOT analysis: Strengths, Weaknesses, Opportunities, Threats
- Goals & Objectives
- Keys to Success
- Summary

After compiling the Executive Summary, the next title is PRESENT STATUS. The Present Status displays the:

- Background: how the business was conceived and by whom
- Progress to Date: discuss what progress has been made to date. For example, if you have a school, discuss the curricula being completed, floor plan drawn, and purchase of land. Discuss what stage the project is in.
- Sales and Marketing: discuss the use of advertising funds, and your demographics identified. Finally list the commonalities shared by your customers.
- Operation & Management: discuss the leadership, their titles and experience. If you have contracted with a management support group, mention that team and their expertise.
- Research & Development: discuss only if there is a need for research and development. This should always be a consideration if you are interested in the global marketplace.
- Financials: discuss any financial support needed and how it will be utilized. If there is a specific bid for vendors etc.

In the PRODUCT/SERVICES section, give specifics about your product and/or services offered. Be specific and discuss intrinsic and extrinsic qualities of the product or service.

Next, what are the KEY FEATURES of the business. This can be displayed under the sub-topic KEY FEATURES and listed in bullet form.

After KEY FEATURES, the next sub-topic is MAIN BENEFITS. Under MAIN BENEFITS list in bullet form the MAIN BENEFITS OFFERED if any.

After MAIN BENEFITS, discuss PRICING PLAN. How is the organization going to price its products or services? Organizations like Sears had a GOOD, BETTER, BEST price point. They distinguished each price point by adding intrinsic qualities to each price point.

While discussing COMPETITIVE ASSESSMENT, it is imperative to know who your competitors are and their strengths and weaknesses.

Under GENERAL BACKGROUND, discuss the entire marketplace. Researching the marketplace is extremely important. For example, for a Chicago business, mention the 6 million population and what percentage will be your organizational focus.

Next SIZE, SEGMENTS AND TRENDS, discuss your hours and work schedule. You may also mention holidays, vacation days etc. Give the reader an idea of when they can come into the business and find it open and available for service. Again, mention your sales plan and future projections. Additionally, discuss which media will be used for advertising.

The fourth or 4.0 portion of the plan is entitled TECHNOLOGY. It should be your goal to have state of the art technology in your state-of-the-art facility. It should be your goal to have state of the art technology in your state-of-the-art facility. If not today, in the future.

The fifth or 5.0 portion is your OPERATIONAL PLANS. Your OPERATIONAL PLANS include the sub-titles LOCATION and FACILITY. If a new construction project, a PROJECTED CONSTRUCTION BUDGET with a square footage cost of $120 - $140 per square foot.

Finally, before you conclude your plan, complete the HUMAN RESOURCE portion of the plan. In this section, discuss how the organization will hire and fire its employees. Remember, your employees are your first customer, and there are laws governing how they should be treated.

Doug McGregor discussed in his research Theory X and Theory Y styles of management how to treat and manage employees. Theory X is managing using coercion and Theory Y is the use of empowerment. Conclusion, the entire plan is summarized in a paragraph or two expressing some important features in the plan.

EXAMPLE OF PROJECTED CONSTRUCTION COST:

Floor area	$40,000 sq. ft
Cost a square ft.	$120
Estimated Construction	$4,800,000
10 % contingency	480,000
Total Estimated Construction Cost	$5,280,000
Price of Space/Land	1,500,000
Projected Purchase & Construction	$6,780,000

CHAPTER V

Developing a Strategic Plan

It is imperative that the organization creates a strategic plan. Like the business plan, it gives directions from where you are, where you want to go, and how you plan to get there. One cannot afford to sail their business in the dark. Knowledge is power!

First do an analysis of where you are in the business. For example, have you determined who the officers and stockholders are and what role will they play?

Will the organization remain in the present city or relocate to a friendlier more productive business environment? All these questions and others need to be answered. Be honest and forthright with your answers.

The first question is WHAT IS? What is the present situation of the organization? Discuss all aspects of the present situation. After answering WHAT IS, ask yourself WHAT SHOULD BE?

To answer WHAT SHOULD BE, one must be a visionary and consider the future. We live in a global business world, and this is one of the questions you need to answer. But caution, while teaching a graduate class in International Business at Chicago's Concordia University-Chicago, I discovered many industries discovered their expenses were more than expected upon relocating to foreign countries.

The factories were in rural areas and far from food

establishments. This meant the employers had to provide food for their employees. Can you say additional expense? Also, they discovered the training offered to employees, due to language barriers etc., they had to teach concepts several times, expense!

Therefore, when the organization considered the global concept, they had to analyze the entire situation through and through. It may be more cost-effective to remain in North America.

The tax base has been one of the biggest complaints of American entrepreneurs and has become an issue to many industries. However, there are states that are business friendly that has little to no state tax. Do your homework!

After answering WHAT IS? WHAT SHOULD BE? The next question is THERE A DISCREPANCY BETWEEN THE TWO? In many instances the answer will be yes, there is a discrepancy between WHAT IS and WHAT SHOULD BE. If there is a discrepancy and a need to develop a business grounded in total quality, that is done through training, obtaining additional capital, facility development, quality marketing and employing individuals who are manageable. Like an athletic team, chemistry plays an important role in the success of the organization. If there is a sin in business, it is not knowing and refusing to ask.

Upon the completion of the questions, the next question IS THERE A QUICK FIX FOR THIS DISCREPANCY? In many instances your answer will be no, there is no quick fix and there is a need for Strategic Planning! If the goal is growth in finances and business growth potential, you need to know there Is No Quick Fix, and a sound structure is needed.

Planning is of utmost importance. Upon completion of the above question, next IS YOUR BUSINESS CLIENT BASED? Well, of course! Every decision in the organization should be client based. If the organization is not serving the client, then why are you in business? Furthermore, it is important that your employees, who are your first client, are treated with the same respect and dignity as your customers.

I recommend researching Doug McGregor's STYLES OF MANGEMENT. He discussed two styles of managing people called Theory X and Theory Y. Theory X is using coercion to manage people and Theory Y deals with empowering people in the workplace. In managing employees, there may be times you may have to use a little coercion, but this should be limited. Most of your managerial focus should be empowerment!

Additionally, the Japanese had a style of management called Theory Z. Theory Z style of management is a style that ties one's home life to their employment. For example, the Japanese frowned on leaving work early to play golf.

In summary, everything the organization does in planning, decision making etc. should be designed to improve service and product for the client.

The next step is IDENTIFY THE PROBLEM. In identifying the problems, they are being made transparent. List the problems honestly and truthfully. Some of the problems the organization may experience are:

- A lack of capital for operations and perhaps construction
- A lack of advertising needed to make our clients aware of our existence
- A need to create a website allowing the clients to purchase online
- A need to purchase office furniture, equipment and maintain a reserve fund
- A need to compile a timetable and campaign for funding

Once the problems are identified, the next question is WHAT ARE YOUR ALTERNATIVE SOLUTIONS? When important problems need a solution, THERE ARE NO ALTERNATIVES.

Next, ARE THE SOLUTIONS GROUNDED IN

RESEARCH? Your solutions should not only be your solutions, but also the solutions of experts. If one is building a school, it is imperative to research and see what Dr. William Glasser, MD, the author of THE QUALITY SCHOOL, QUALITY SCHOOL TEACHER, and REALITY THERAPY has to say, or my research AN HISTORICAL CASE STUDY OF A QUALITY SCHOOL. In this research I took a group of Chicago students for three years from at risk to the Most Improved 8th grade Reading Class in all of Cook County (Chicago Tribune, November 1998). Chicago is in Cook County.

After all the above questions have been significantly answered, it is IMPLEMENTATION time. The solutions should be implemented with the idea that one is opened to re-evaluation at any time. With the uniqueness of culture, fickle economies and other reasons, global business is often changing. One cannot be shy when it comes to re-evaluating the organization.

Once IMPLEMENTATION is completed, you are ready to analyze your progress. A system should be in place for evaluating how the business is moving forward, and what changes, if any, should be made.

While working for Sears Headquarters in Chicago, I was appalled to discover, senior management was often too slow in evaluating situations and making the necessary changes. What was more appalling was, being a senior manager was the stumbling block that kept them from including brand name products in their stores for years. For many years, they only carried products made specifically for the Sears brand. When the Senior Vice President made his transition, the next day they had national brand name products on the shelves.

Also, working in the Furniture Buying Department, there was a sub-line of furniture made specifically for the African American and Latino customer. At least that is what they thought. Being one of two African Americans salaried in the Department, I thought it would be valuable input when I told them, "my friends and family would not buy those products". Well, they ignored it, and the line was later terminated. The products did not produce the dollars they projected. Preparing a Strategic Plan that the organization could give their input and be proud of.

STRATEGIC PLAN

I.   What is?

II.   What should be?

III.   Is there a discrepancy between what is and what should be?

IV.   Is there a quick fix?

V.   Is the business client based?

VI.   Identify the problems

VII.   What are the alternatives?

VIII. What are possible solutions to problems?

IX.   Are the problems grounded in research?

X.   Implementation

XI.   Evaluation & Re-evaluation

CHAPTER VI

Creating the 5 Year Budget

Using Excel, the heading across the top of the page should include the name of the business, address, email address, telephone number. Under that the information should include the number of employees projected to be hired and the projected 5-year budget total.

The budget is divided into three sections. Section 1 employee job title and salaries. For example, the CEO of the company will make $100,000 a year. Next to the title CEO there is a quantity column that would show the number 1.

Column 2 heading is Salary where the $100,000 is shown. This amount is shown in columns 1 through 5 meaning the CEO will make $100,000 for the next 5 years. The same procedure is used for the following employees:

Title	Qty.	Salaries	Year 1	Year 2	Year 3	Year 4	Year 5
CEO	1	100,000	100,000	100,000	100,00	100,000	100,000
VP	2	75,000	75,000	75,000	75,000	75,000	75,000

Follow the same procedure for the other positions in Section 1 marked Salaries all the way down to the Parking Attendants. Upon completion of listing the titles and salaries, total each column, HIGHLIGHT EACH COLUMN, CLICK ON THE

BACKWARD 3 IN THE UPPER RIGHT COLUMN TO TOTAL THE COLUMN.

Section 2 is titled FRINGE BENEFITS. This column is completed in the same manner as Section 1. Under this section, write incentives and total the employees. Upon writing Incentives, choose the percentage (5%). For example:

Title	Qty.	Year 1	Year 2	Year 3	Year 4	Year 5
Fringe	130	2,000,000	2,000,000	2,000,000	2,000,000	2,000,000

Incentives: 5%

To finalize the FRINGE BENEFIT column, take 5% of the fringe benefits for each year, and record in each column at the bottom. For example, 5% of $2,000,000 is $100,000. Record that $100,000 under the $2,000,000 column.

Before getting to the final section called EXPENSES, under each of the five columns ESTIMATE YOUR TAXES. Determine from your Certified Public Accountant your tax percentage. This percentage may be 20%, 25% or less.

Under Fringe Benefits and Incentives, write Estimated Taxes. Follow this procedure for each column beginning with Year 1. For example, Estimated Taxes using 20%, take 20% of years 1-5 and record the amounts for each column. Example, 20% of $2,000,000 is $400,000. Complete the same calculation for the other years.

Total the total salaries, fringe benefits, incentives and taxes to get a TOTAL SALARIES & FRINGE BENEFITS. Now that all the columns have been totaled, the next move is to RECORD THE OPERATION EXPENSES. Those expenses used in the operation of the business, office supplies, marketing expense, medical clinic budget, electricity etc.

PROGRAM EXPENSES is the heading for this last section. Under column 1 write the Expense Name, then the expense amount for each of the five years. Total the PROGRAM EXPENSE column for each of the 5-years and add those totals to the previous title totals above for a yearly GRAND TOTAL.

Remember to total the columns, HIGHLIGHT EACH COLUMN, CLICK ON THE BACKWARD 3 IN THE UPPER RIGHT-HAND CORNER OF THE EXCEL PROGRAM TO TOTAL THAT COLUMN.

CHAPTER VII

Developing a Balance Sheet

In computing the net worth of a business, use the formula Assets=liabilities + owner's equity. Assets are those things you own, your home, car, clothing etc. In business, assets are cash, accounts receivable (customers who owe) car, insurance etc.

To have any net worth, monies or things that are left after all debts or liabilities are paid. Let us assume there is a million dollars in assets. Remember assets include cash, accounts receivable, machinery, buildings, equipment etc.

Liabilities are those individuals you owe. A liability account ends with the word Payable. Accounts Payable. Again, a liability is a creditor you owe. There are Current Liabilities, which includes Account Payable, Taxes Payable, Notes Payable. The next is Long Term Liabilities which includes Bank Notes Payable.

The Owner's Equity may be called COMMON OR PREFERRED STOCK of the business. The Owner's Equity is still the amount that is left after all liabilities are paid. Assets-Liabilities=Owner's Equity.

The Owner's Equity is important for the continued existence of the business. In closing, remember to learn this accounting formula: Assets= Liabilities + Owner's Equity. Thanks to Morgan Park High School in Chicago, I learned this formula early in my high school career.

Let us say you have a $1,000,000 in assets and two hundred thousand in liabilities, your net worth is $800,000.

$1,000,000 - $200,000 = $800,000 net worth

On the balance sheet, the assets are usually the lead-off man on the balance sheet. In a vertical balance sheet, it appears at the top of the page. In a horizontal balance sheet, the assets appear on the left side of the balance sheet and the liabilities and net worth on the right-hand side of the balance sheet.

Under the head ASSETS appears CURRENT ASSETS, cash, accounts receivable, prepare insurance etc.

Under CURRENT ASSETS, the next heading is FIXED ASSETS. FIXED ASSETS include machinery, equipment, buildings.

CHAPTER VIII

Compiling an Income Statement

In business, the income statement contains the income earned and the expenses paid out. Monies earned in the operation of selling products or services are called income and recorded on this statement.

Income is often expressed on the income statement as Sales, Revenue and Income. The income account may appear in the accounting ledger with the digit 4 in front of the word Income.

The statement starts with Income and is followed on the income statement by the word Expenses. The expense accounts begin with the digit 5 and each individual expense, paid by the company is recorded. For example, Salary Expense may be shown as 51.

Upon finishing the recording of the different expenses, the expense column is totaled, and that amount is subtracted from the Income Total. That total is called GROSS PROFIT BEFORE TAXES. The taxes due are subtracted from GROSS PROFIT BEFORE TAXES to get Net Income.

The Income Total or Net Income is recorded in the ledger in the income account showing the net amount earned for that period.

For example, the Salary Expense is recorded in the ledger under the Salary Expense account as a debit. The debit in expense accounts represent a decrease in income. In other words, instead of debiting the credit account income, it is posted in each individual expense account as a debit. All expenses carry a debit balance, and the income account carries a credit balance.

When the credit side of the income account which carries a credit, balance is more than the debit side of all expense accounts, there is a Profit. Diametrically, when there are more expenses than the income account, there is a Loss!

XYZ CORPORATION

INCOME STATE

DECEMBER 31, 2018

INCOME:

SALES		500,000
EXPENSES:		
Salary Expense	2,000	
Utility Expense	1,000	
Insurance Expense	500	
Automobile Expense	1,000	
	_____	
Total Expenses		4,500
		_____
Gross Profit Before Taxes		495,500
20% Taxes Due		99,100
Net Income		396,400
		_____
		_____

CHAPTER IX

Completing the Articles of Incorporations

A corporation will protect the owner in a for-profit business. When considering sole proprietorship, partnership and corporation, the corporation is the only business structure whereby the owner's personal assets cannot be touched if the business debt is more than the business assets. In other words, if the business debt is $50,000 and they have only $40,000 in assets, the extra $10,000 may be taken from the owner's personal assets if they are a sole proprietorship or partnership, but not a corporation.

In completing the Article of Incorporation, get the paperwork from the Secretary of State website and search out the sub-title Business. In Illinois after going to the Secretary of State website, under Service, click on the sub-title Business and choose your function.

In the Search Box type ARTICLES OF INCORPORATION. One can prepay online, which is more expensive because the process is expedited. The extra fee may be around a $100 or more, however, the organization will receive the paperwork in a shorter time.

If time is extremely important, you may complete it online. When preparing Illinois form BCA2.10 follow these easy steps:

Item 1. Corporate Name

Type the name of the business followed by the word Corporation, Company, Incorporated, Limited.

Item 2.

Complete the name, address, city, state, zip code, and county of Registered Agent. This could very well be you.

Item 3.

State the purpose for which the corporation is organized. If not on the form, type "For the transaction of any or all lawful business for which corporations may be incorporated under the Illinois (your state) business corporate act".

Item 4.

Authorized shares issued shares and consideration received. In other words, what are the authorized shares and if you will issue a portion or all the shares, and the consideration or proceeds received from the shares.

IMPORTANT: the number of shares issued may affect the amount of fee paid to the state. It may be better to choose 6,000 shares at a dollar per share.

Class # of shares authorized shares to be issued consideration

Common 6,000 6,000 $6,000

Under Class type Common Stock, Under # of shares authorized type 6,000, for shares issued type 6,000 and consideration $6,000.

Item 5.

List the number of directors. We suggest an odd number like 3 or 5. List their names and addresses.

Item 6.

Type N/A. There is no need to offer additional information.

Item 7.

Type names, addresses of directors and their signatures. The signatures must be in Black ink on the original document. Remember to submit the original in duplicate with fee.

Note: the fee schedule is based on the initial franchise tax being assessed at the rate of 15/100 of 1% ($1.50 per $1,000) on the paid in capital represented in the state.

The minimum initial franchise tax is $25 in some states. The filing fee is $150. The minimum total due is $175 in Illinois.

Return to Portion:

Type name of corporation, agent's name and agent address. Your stamped copy will be returned to this individual. KEEP IN SAFE PLACE.

CHAPTER X

A Management Guide for Business

The function of management is deciding the best way to use a company's resources to provide the best goods and services to the customer.

A good manager must be capable of:

- Communicating well with employees
- Making good competent decisions
- Having excellent and strong planning skills
- Assigning work to employees knowing who is best qualified to complete the task
- Knowing to train and motivate team members
- Being objective in appraising employees

To date, management is more challenging due to changes in the workplace such as technology, diversity in the workplace, global economies etc.

Companies of different sizes and purpose need managers and may have several levels such as senior, middle and supervisory management.

SENIOR MANAGEMENT

Senior management is the highest level of management in the chain. It includes CEO, CMOs, and COOs. Senior management is not involved in day-to-day problems and situations, but in setting goals and objectives for the company.

MIDDLE MANAGEMENT

Senior management sets the goals and objectives and middle management meet those goals. Examples of middle management is district managers and department heads.

SUPERVISORY MANAGEMENT

Supervisory management is responsible for day to day operation of the company and are known as front line managers. Examples of supervisory management are crew leaders and forepersons.

ASSESSING MANAGEMENT

The management process must be assessed, and this is done in several ways. They can be assessed in:

- Set of behaviors & roles
- Abilities to do the job and their skills
- In the task they perform

| MANAGEMENT TASK

There are basically several tasks performed by managers:

- Planning – deciding goals and actions to be taken by company
- Organizing – Assigning and organizing task to employees
- Staffing – Recruit and train employees for the task
- Controlling – Measuring and evaluating the performance of the company
- Leading – Providing necessary guidance to staff as needed.

Managers are called to be in the moment but are also called upon to focus on long-term goals and objectives.

Managerial skills include decision making, human relations and technical skills. Technical skills are specific abilities needed to perform the job. Human relation skills are needed to work well with people of different skills and background. For years, employers have complained about workers not being able to work well in teams. In coordinating the decision making and long-term planning skills, it is paramount that different departments work well together. Because employees are the company's first customer, they must be treated with the utmost of respect.

Also, author Doug McGregor in his publication Theory X, Y & Z discussed the need for empowerment when it comes to trusting and working employees. Theory X is managing using coercion, this style of management is not good unless necessary for a specific action. Employees are turned off when they are treated and disrespected. Theory Y is managing using empowerment. Employees are empowered and trusted to complete an assignment with trust and quality in a timely manner.

Also, author Ouch suggested a style of management known as Theory Z. Mr. Ouch discussed the eastern culture, like Japan, has a style of management that also includes the employee's home life. For example, if an employee leaves work early to play golf, the family views that behavior as disrespectful.

Finally, many managers today look upon these styles as too simplistic and a broader approach may be in order. Other managers believe empowering employees is appropriate and allows their actions and conduct determine if a change is necessary.

CHAPTER XI

Communication Skills for Business

Communication is an exchange of information. The information is used to instruct, command, persuade and influence others in the workplace.

Good communication skills are needed to manage people. Managers use communication every day, and many believe, 75 percent of the time in business is spent communicating. Good managers want to develop good communication skills. Communication is used to motivate employees and communicate effectively and clearly.

Communication is important because:

- Managers must be able to persuade employees in the workplace
- Managers must be able to understand and absorb other employee ideas
- Managers must give good clear information to motivate and instruct employees
- Managers must convince their customers to do repeated business with their company.

Interpersonal communication is extremely important. It involves an interactive process between two or more people to send and receive information. This communication could be verbal communication or non-verbal communication. It is imperative that we understand and are being understood. In texting, it is easy to misinterpret a message. The tone could be misinterpreted.

Semantics is the science of studying the meaning of words, and to realize that some words mean different things. For example, the word "to" is a preposition, the other "too" is an adverb and the number "two" signifies how many. When spoken, the individual receiving the message must distinguish between the three.

Our emotions at the time we communicate (send or receive messages) affect the message. Several years ago, while working in radio, a listener called an informed me that I was communicating to my audience that I was upset. Well, she was totally correct. On the way to the studio, my then wife and I exchanged words and it carried over into my on-air-performance.

In learning to communicate, it is imperative to:

- Understand the audience
- Develop good listening skills
- Give clear feedback
- Be conscious of our non-verbal self when communicating.

In understanding the audience, it is imperative to know who is being spoken to and why.

Develop good listening skills, it helps the manager absorb information, understands others and their point of view, and aid in recognizing possible problems. In listening to the sender, be careful, careful not to frame your answer prior to hearing the complete statement. Do not do this!

Be aware of your purpose, ideas and body language in giving a clear feedback. Also, be careful to give an appropriate response to the question or statement.

Finally, be aware and careful and conscious of your body language and non-verbal communication. While speaking, one should be award and conscious of the pitch, temp, loudness and hesitation while speaking. Additionally, be conscious and aware of your physical distance to the receiver, and your eye contact. It plays a role in your delivery and supplements your verbal communication.

Oral and written communication are forms of communication with others. In written communication:

- Being effective at written communication is a must for managers
- Managers must remember to keep their communication clear and simple
- Being aware of the content and tone of speech is important for managers
- Always proofread your written content prior to delivery.

Also, in oral communication"

- Your presentation must be persuasive and informal
- It should be used to give motivation and clear instructions.

When developing oral communication skills,

- Avoid monotone
- Make emotional contact with the other party
- Be as enthusiastic and positive as possible
- Do not interrupt the individual speaking
- Be courteous and polite
- While speaking, avoid words such as like, and, um and uh!

Determine the best method of communication. Written communication is best for routine information, and for sensitive information verbal communication may be the best avenue.

| COMMUNICATING WITHIN AN ORGANIZATION

Within the organization the (1) email, (2) intranet, (3) grapevine and (4) networking may be used:

The email is an electronic way of communicating with others. It is high speed exchange of written information but is believed to be open to misinformation and emotions.

The intranet is a private network used by corporations. It uses internet technologies and is usually internal.

The grapevine Is an informal form of communicating with co-workers, friends and strangers. It is a form manager use to communicate information. People are often challenged to be careful because information could be changed or misinterpreted.

Poor management communication could lead to corporate mistakes and bunders, therefore, be careful! In communicating, be aware of the culture of the information you are communicating with and be aware how communication changes from culture to culture. In communicating from culture to culture, avoid slang and write and speak clearly.

CHAPTER XII

Obtaining an Employer Identification Number

In setting up a business account at the bank, the business will need an Employer Identification Number or EIN.

The Employer Identification Number, EIN, for a checking account is the same as the social security number for your daily use. When applying for the business EIN on the www.irs.gov website, the form may be completed online.

In the search box, click on the box at the top of the page and type EIN. After clicking on the top of the page to get the EIN, drop down to the bottom of the page where it says APPLY ONLINE. A list of businesses will appear. Click on Business and kinds of businesses will appear. This is also true if you choose to apply for a Trust Account.

Complete the information in the box using your name, address and social security number. The system will only allow one application a day. If you attempt a second in the second day, your social security number alerts them that you have already completed one that day.

Answer the question: IS THIS AN INDIVIDUAL OR EXISTING BUSINESS. If the EIN is used for a new business, click individual. Next, choose between printing out the information or having it mailed to you. I suggest printing out and click on the logo under the question to complete printing the official pages.

You are now prepared to take your EIN to the bank to get your new checking account.

For a non-profit business, a non-interest checking account is suggested. This prevents the business from paying interest on the account when the business receives a 1099 from the bank at the end of the year. When going to the bank, you will need to take:

- Articles of Incorporation papers
- EIN
- Some cash. Probably $50.

CHAPTER XIII

Intellectual Properties & How to Handle it

Intellectual properties include patents, trademarks, copyrights, trade secrets and represents important assets and should the management have some understanding of intellectual properties before approaching an attorney.

All business is regulated by law and a new for an attorney is of utmost importance. The need for understanding all regulations are also important to the company.

In selecting an attorney, select one who not only knows the law but specific areas of the law as well. A competent attorney should understand the law and all possible circumstances/outcomes pertaining to the law.

In hiring an attorney, they should be somebody you can work with and relate to. A good relationship with the attorney increases one's ability to have a better outcome.

| PATENTS

A contract between the government and an inventor is called a patent. The government grants the inventor exclusivity in exchange for disclosure of the invention. This exclusivity is granted for a specific amount of time. At the end of the time, it becomes a part of the public domain and is published by the government.

The utility patent, which is what most people are referring to when discussing patents, has a 20-year term beginning on the date of filing with the Patent and Trademark Office. The fees are based on the number of claims made in the patent application.

A utility patent grants the owner protection from anyone else making, selling or using the identified invention and often reflects protection of new, useful and unobvious processes such as film developing, photocopiers, composition of matter such as chemical compounds and mixtures of ingredients. Also, articles of manufacture such as the toothpaste pump.

| DESIGN PATENTS

A design patent reflects the appearance of an objective. This covers new, original, ornamental, and unobvious designs for articles of manufacture. They are granted for a 14-year term and provides, like the utility patent, the inventor with a negative right excluding other from making, selling and using the patent.

The initial filing fee for the design patent is in the range of $110 for a small entity. There are other fees such as issuance fee, depending on the size of the item.

| PLANT PATENTS

The plant patent is issued under the same provision as the utility patent and are for new varieties of plants. They represent a limited area of interest, and very few are issued.

INTERNATIONAL PATENTS

It has become important for US companies to seek protection in global markets and the need for an International Patent has increased.

With the concern for knock-offs International Patents have become increasing important for start-up businesses. To facilitate this, the Patent Cooperation Treat (PCT) with over 142 participants was established to facilitate the filing process in multiple countries. This is done in one office rather than filing in each separate country, and is done in Geneva, Switzerland and provides a preliminary search for possible infringements in any country.

It is recommended that the entrepreneur files a Provisional Patent Application to establish a date of conception of the invention. This replaces the disclosure document that the PTO previously accepted.

In addition, the new provisional application is consistent with the European procedures and can be critical for a foreign company. This application gives the entrepreneur a first to file right.

THE PATENT APPLICATION

The patent application can be downloaded from the Patent and Trademark office website and must contain a complete history and description of the invention and claims for its usefulness. The form is divided into sections:

- Introduction – It should clearly state how the invention differs from existing projects and should contain background information and advantages for its usefulness.

- Description of Invention – All drawings must comply with PTO requirements and must contain a brief description of all enclosed drawings. The draws may include engineering specifications, materials, components that are vital to the actual making of the invention and should include a detailed description of the invention.
- Claims – Claims are the criteria by which any infringements will be determined. Essential parts of the invention are described in broad terms and serve to specify what the entrepreneur is trying to patent. Additionally, the application should contain an oath or declaration that is signed by the inventor or inventors. The attorney may supply this form and the completed form is sent to the PTO, and the status of the invention is patent pending. The patent is then published and becomes accessible to the public for review. The files will vary based upon the patent search and claims made. The attorney files are factored in completing the application. If you choose to file online, use the EFS Web service provided by PTO. Some believe there are advantage to file online.

PATENT INFRINGEMENT

Many businesses, inventions, or innovations are the result of improvements on or modification to existing products and is imperative for the entrepreneur to be sensitive about infringing on someone else's patent.

It may be good business strategy to copy and improve on a product and may be perfectly legal to do so. If there is an infringement, the entrepreneur may try to license the product from the patent holder.

BUSINESS METHOD PATENTS

Some firms who hold Business Method Patents have used them to assault competitors and to provide a steady stream of income from royalties or licensing fees. With the growth of software development etc. has emerged the use of business method patents. Amazon and its single click feature used by customers is an example.

START-UP WITHOUT A PATENT

Not every start-up business will have a concept that is patentable. Being first in the market may be an advantage over competitors. However, being able to maintain this advantage is an asset or advantage to the business. It may be difficult but would be advantageous to the existence of the start-up.

TRADEMARKS

A distinguished word, name or symbol used to identify a product is a Trademark. It may be a sound, word, symbol etc. to identify the source or sponsorship of a good or service.

A trademark, unlike the patent, can last indefinitely. It can last if it continues to perform a function. Trademarks filed after November 16, 1989 are given an initial 10-year registration with another 10-renewable term. In the middle of this term or the 5th year, the registrant is required to file an affidavit with the PTO indicating it is in commercial use. It is canceled if not filed. In the 9th or 10th year after registration, every 10 years thereafter, an application for renewal must be filed. If not filed, it is canceled. The registrant is given a 6-month grace period.

TRADEMARK REGISTRATION

To file an application, the entrepreneur must complete a simple form that can be downloaded and submitted by mail or filed electronically using the Trademark Electronic Application System (TEAS) on the PTO website.

The following four requirements must be met:

- Completion of written form
- A drawing of the mark
- Five specimens showing the actual use of the product
- Enclosing the fee.

Remember, each trademark must be applied for separately. The PTO, upon receipt, will assign a serial number to the application and send the applicant a filing receipt.

The examining attorney at the PTO will determine the suitability for registration. This suitability will be made within 3 months. If there is an objection by the entrepreneur, it must be made within 6 months or the application is considered abandoned. The right to appeal is still available if made to the PTO.

The trademark, if accepted, is published in the Trademark Official Gazette, allowing any party 30 days opposing or requesting an extension to oppose. If there is no opposition, it is filed, and the registration is issued. This process usually takes up to 13 months from the initial filing.

COPYRIGHTS

The copyright does not protect the idea itself and allows someone else to use the idea or concept in a different manner, but it protects the original works of the author. With the expansion of the internet the copyright law has become relevant today.

Copyrights are registered with the Library of Congress and may not require an attorney. To register, the applicant must send an application of $35 if filed online or $45 if filed by mail. No other fees may apply based on the number of works included. Go to www.copyright.gov for further information. Copyrights are suitable for such things as computer software, books, scripts, articles, poems, songs, sculpture, models, maps, blueprints, collages, printed material on board games, date and music.

LICENSING

An arrangement between two parties where one party has proprietary rights over some information, process, or technology protected by a trademark, copyright or patent. The licensee is required, as stated in the contract, to pay a royalty or some other sum to the holder in return for permission to copy the copyright, trademark or patent.

A patent license agreement specifies how the licensee would have access to the patent and in case of a trademark generally involves a franchising agreement. An amount is usually determined for the use.

CONTRACT

A contract is a legally enforceable agreement between two or more parties with certain with certain conditions.

Some of those conditions are:

- An offer made and voluntary acceptance of that offer
- Consideration: value given by both parties
- Contract must be legal
- Any amount of $50 or more must be in writing.

| CONTRACT BREACH

The party breaching the contract must pay damages or live up to the terms of the contract. If one fails to live up to the terms, the other party can drop the matter and not live up to their end of the contract. In large transactions, it is advisable to hire an attorney.

CHAPTER XIV

Filing Chapter 7 Bankruptcy

File Chapter 7 Bankruptcy is a step by step process. Initially, take the pretest online for $25. For further test information, contact Financial Educational Services.

You will need your social security card. If you do not have one, contact your local Social Security Office in your area and obtain one. The attorney will expect you to have one for the hearing.

Obtain two years of income tax returns to take to the hearing. If you do not have them, contact the Internal Revenue Service online or contact the office that serves your home state. This is also needed for the hearing.

Next, obtain 2-3 months of bank statements from your bank. Also, compile a list of all creditors you owe. List their names, addresses and amount owed. Make sure you type this information, so it is readable.

The forms needed for the Chapter 7 Bankruptcy can be obtained at the local Federal Building in your district:

- (Official Form 6A) (12/07) Schedule A – Real Property

List any real properties you own, the bank, and current value

- (Official Form 6B) (12/07) Schedule B – Personal Property

List all personal property you own from bank accounts to household goods, including clothing etc. If you do not own a specific piece of personal property listed, IN THE BOX MARKED "X" FOR NONE.

- (Official Form 6C) (04/10) Schedule C – Property Claimed as Exempt. List all household goods, furniture, clothing etc.
- Official Form 6D) (12/07 Schedule D – Creditors Holding Secured Claims. This may include first or second mortgages on any real properties, secured loans etc. List the name of the company, address, date incurred, amount, account number, add the column and total at the bottom.
- (Official Form 6E) (04/10 Schedule E – Creditors holding Unsecured Priority Claim. Complete this form and note in the middle of the page, there is a box to check if debtor has no creditors holding unsecured priority claims to report on this schedule.
- (Official Form 6F) (12/07) Schedule F – Creditors Holding Unsecured Nonpriority Claims. List all charge cards, date claim was incurred and amounts. After listing, total bottom of page.
- (Official Form 6G) (12/07) Schedule G – Executory Contracts and Unexpired Leases. Use this form if you have leases outstanding or contracts. If not, check the box that says you have no executor contracts or unexpired leases.
- (Official Form 6J) (12/07) Schedule J – Current Expenditures of Individual Debtor(s). List on this form your mortgage payment, food, clothing etc. Please complete in pencil then trace in ink. Total column at the bottom of page.

- B7 (Official Form 7) (04/10) Titled: United States Bankruptcy Court. Include all income from employment and or business. If not check the box that states NONE. Also, review pages 2-10 and check individual boxes.
- B 22A (Official Form 22A) Chapter 7) (12/10) Chapter 7 Statement of Current Monthly Income and Means-Test Calculation. This form must be completed by every individual Chapter 7 debtor. Part 1 Military Individual, Part 2 Income Exclusion etc.
- Form 6 – Statistical Summary (12/07) United States Bankruptcy Court; Statistical Summary. Finally, if you live in the Northern District of Illinois, you and your attorney will file your paperwork with Kenneth S. Gardner, Clerk or his replacement. There is a fee of about $350 to file and you will appear before the Trustee who will ask you a series of questions. Take your social security card, bank statements an income tax return.

CHAPTER XV

Succession Planning & Ending the Venture

Every entrepreneur needs an exit plan. Exit strategy include an initial public offering (IPO), private sale of stock, succession by a family member or a nonfamily member, liquidation of company, merger with another company.

The sale of the company could be to an external source or to the employees. Each has its advantages and disadvantages. The most important thing is the entrepreneur has a plan in place at the start-up stage instead of waiting until it might be too late to implement an option. Unfortunately, only 60% of businesses have a succession plan, and when it comes to small businesses, even less.

▌ TIPS FOR SUCCESSION

- Start early allowing enough time for the process
- Estimate the company's value
- Evaluate potential successors on their merit
- If considering a family member, make sure they have the skills and motivation to do the task
- Allow the successor to learn the business by providing a transition period

- For a management succession, consider options like employee stock option plans
- Set a completion date and stick to it.

If a family member is not interested, it is imperative to sell the business or train someone within the company to take over.

| TRANSFERRING BUSINESS TO FAMILY MEMBER

It is believed passing the business, successfully, to a family member is a tough task. Research the Family Business Institute for further statistics. It is believed that only 30 percent of family businesses survive into the second generation and 12 percent survive into the third generation. With these statistics, the need for a succession plan is evident.

Furthermore, an effective succession plan should be made know to employees. This is extremely important for those employees who may be affected by the transition.

In creating an effective succession plan, it is necessary to consider:

- The transition position of the owner. Will he/she work full time, part time or retire
- The family dynamics. Are there members of the family who are unable or unwilling to work together?
- The income for working family members and shareholders
- What is the business environment during transition?
- What are the tax consequences during transition?

Caution, the transfer of a business to a family member can create internal problems with employees. This may result when a son and daughter is handed the responsibility or running the business without adequate training.

In the case of a young family member they should assume various operational responsibilities early in the business. Rotating to different departments, as in an internship, gives them a good perspective of the total operation of the business.

Additionally, the entrepreneur staying around to act as an advisor to the successor, may be a wise idea.

▌TRANSFER TO NONFAMILY MEMBERS

When a family member is not interested in assuming responsibility for the business, often you have three choices. Retain control and hire a manager, sell the business outright or train a key employee and retain some equity.

Passing the business on to an employee keeps an individual in place who is familiar with the business and the marketplace. This may also minimize transitional problems and allows the entrepreneur to take time in the transition process.

Ownership is the key issue in passing the business on to an employee. If the entrepreneur plans to retain some ownership, the question is how much becomes an area of negotiation. The new owner may desire the entrepreneur to remain a consultant, stockholder or minority owner. To give you ample time to make the transition, begin the process with plenty of time to complete it in plenty of time.

▌OPTIONS FOR SELLING THE BUSINESS

- Direct Sale – This is probably the most common method for selling the business. The owner retires or moves on to some other venture. In this process, you may choose to use a broker who will receive a commission. Using a business plan or a five-year plan can give the buyer a glance into the future.

- Employee Stock Option Plan – This plan allows the entrepreneur to sell the business to employees over time. The employee stock option establishes a trust that borrows against future profits. It is estimated in the United States, there are about 11,500 Employee Stock Option Plan companies. Of that total, 3,000 are wholly owned by the Employee Stock Option Plan. Some disadvantages are it is quite complex to establish, and it requires a complete valuation of the venture in establishing an amount of the ESOP package.

- Management Buyout – Management buyouts usually involve a direct sale for a predetermined price. This is like selling a house. An appraisal of all assets plus the goodwill must be established. Included in that process is also the past revenue or income of the business.

   Selling to employees can be financed in several ways including a cash sell. If the business is substantial, a cash sale is unlikely. Another method is through a public offering or a merger with another business. The major decision will depend on the goals of the entrepreneur.

- Bankruptcy – It has been reported that half of the businesses fail in the first year. Failure is not unusual in many new ventures. Bankruptcies run nearly 2 million per year. Chapter 7 is the most common type of business bankruptcy. Liquidation is also a common form accounting for 70 percent of the total in some fiscal years. Chapter 11 bankruptcy provides an opportunity for a business to reorganize, regroup and prepare a new business plan approved by the courts.

CHAPTER XVI

Establishing a Business Boot-Camp

Today, in the twenty-first century America has fallen behind globally in entrepreneurship. While reading "Inside Wealth" a diagram was displayed showing where the world is on business start-ups.

To my surprise, America was last with 21 percent, behind South Africa 68 percent, Latin America 58 percent, Asia-Pacific 57 percent, Middle East 48 percent, Europe 41 percent and lastly America 21 percent.

I knew something had to be done, and in the spirit of entrepreneurship, I received a vision for this mentoring program. Like in professional baseball, a minor league system must be established to train the young and old.

ADMINISTRATIVE

| COORDINATOR & CO-CORDINATOR

The coordinator oversees the day to day activities of the program. The individual visits each individual area and coordinates all activities needed for the program to run smoothly.

| MISSION STATEMENT

The Wall Street Business Boot-Camp intends to introduce new mentees to the business environment with the hope that one day they will entertain the thought of becoming an entrepreneur.

| VISION STATEMENT

The vision is to expand this program into other regions and countries in hope to create positions and opportunities that will allow populations to improve business opportunities in their communities and countries, and to grow businesses everywhere.

| PROJECT MOTTO

I see the vision, I am motivated to act, the future is up to me!

| GOALS

- Introduce business concepts and practices to mentees at an early age through the country and world

- Hands on learning opportunities
- Build an interest and desire to become an entrepreneur.

MENTEES

The mentees are students attending from 12 and up enrolled in the program. The program is divided into three classes, Class A, Class AA and Class AAA.

MENTORS

Those individuals overseeing each activity. In many instances, they should have some experience in business via a degree, working in business etc.

ASSISTANTS

Assistants are those individuals assisting the mentors in the classroom or each individual division.

PAYROLL

For those individuals who have sponsors and paid programs, the mentors and staff will be paid at the end of the program. For those individuals who do not have sponsors or paid programs, please ignore.

| TUTORS

For those individuals who have difficulty with reading and writing, a tutoring program will be done prior to the beginning of the program. This area of the Camp is elective.

| SUGGESTED PROGRAM TERM

Spring Term – March – May, Saturday classes
Summer Term – June-August, Saturday classes
Fall Term – September – November, Saturday classes
December – Christmas & Holiday break
Each term will meet Saturdays from 9:00 am to 1:00 pm.
8:30 – 9:00 Mentors Briefing
9:00 – Snack OPTIONAL
9:30 – Beginning of Classes
11:30 – 11:40 Beverage Break OPTIONAL
11:40 – Continue in class
1:00 – Dismissal with MOTTO
MOTTO: I SEE THE VISION, I'M MOTIVATED TO ACT, THE FUTURE IS UP TO ME!

| ATTENDANCE

To achieve the goals and objectives of this program, and for the mentees to get the full learning experience intended, it is imperative for the mentees to be prompt at every section.

Only one absence, without a doctor's excuse per term is acceptable. Too many absences, and the mentee will be dismissed until the beginning of next session.

▌RESEARCH PAPER

Written in:

1. American Psychological Association style with references in the body of the paper. For example:
   William Glasser, MD in <u>The Quality School</u> (1989) stated fun, safety, and love should be included in the learning experience.
2. Font 12 single spaced
3. Written in block style
4. Cover Sheet showing – name of business, mentees' name and minor league level
5. Body of paper – Historical literature, relevant theories, current literature, conclusion, references
6. Between 5 – 10 pages

▌RULES

1. Prompt attendance
2. Mutual respect for all
3. No hats or caps in facility
4. Keep areas clean
5. Other rules as necessary

▌POSSIBLE LOCATIONS

1. Fieldhouse & Park Districts
2. Churches
3. Schools

RECOMMENDED READINGS

1. Think & Grow Rich
2. The 7 Habits of Highly Effective People
3. Rich Dad Poor Dad
4. Think Big
5. The Richest Man in Babylon

MINOR LEAGUE BUSINESS SYSTEM

| CLASS A – ELEMENTARY

CHAPTER: 1 INFORMATION FOR ENTREPRENEURS

Week 1.

Opening: I SEE THE VISION, I'M MOTIVATED TO ACT, THE FUTURE IS UP TO ME.
Lecture: Chapter 1
Discussion: Question and answer period about Entrepreneurship.
Research: Discuss research paper written in American Psychological Association style of research with reference in body of paper. Example: William, Glasser, MD in The Quality School (1989) stated fun, safety, and love should be included in the learning experience.

Allow students to choose a business industry to research. Inform mentees once they choose, they cannot change; therefore, give it serious consideration.

Week 2.

Lecture: Review Week 1 and conclude chapter 1.
Discussion: Questions and answer session pertaining to entrepreneurship
Research: Mentees will work on research papers. Also, allow them to choose one partner for the project. No more than two per project. They will share work and credit.

Week 3.

Lecture: Chapter on Business Plan
Discussion: Questions and answers concerning writing a business plan.
Research: Mentees will work on research papers in preparation for mounting on three-sided boards for Business Fair.

Week 4.

Lecture: Complete business plan lecture.
Research: Mentees continue to work on research projects.
Months: April
Chapter: Strategic Plan

Week 1.

Lecture: Strategic Plan
Discussion: Question and answer on Strategic Planning
Research: Mentees continue working on research paper

Week 2.

Lecture: Discussion on 5-year Budget
Discussion: Questions and answers about 5-year Budget
Research: Mentees continue working on industry paper, business plan strategic plan and 5-year Budget

Week 3.

Lecture: Review Week 2 topic on 5-year Budget
Discussion: Questions and answers
Research: Mentees continue working on research papers etc.

Week 4.

Lecture: Chapter on Balance Sheets
Discussion: Question & answer session about Balance Sheets
Research: Mentees continue research papers on chosen industry and begin mounting their three-sided project boards. See board mounting.

NEW SESSION:

Lecture: Chapter on Income Statements

Week 1.

Lecture: Review all precious discussions
Discussion: Questions & answer session
Research: Mentees will type research papers in APA style.

Week 2.

Lecture: Continue Reviewing Previous Sessions
Mentees will continue working on projects.

Week 3.

Mentees will continue to finalize mounting projects & practicing presentations.

Week 4.

Mentees will continue working on their projects and practicing their presentations.

The Business Fair will be scheduled for an evening to allow the parents, guardians and friends to attend.

CLASS AA – HIGH SCHOOL (AGE)

| POSSIBLE MONTHS – MARCH, JUNE, SEPTEMBER

Opening: I SEE THE VISION, I'M MOTIVATED TO ACT, THE FUTURE IS UP TO ME!

If possible, show HIDDEN COLORS the first visit

Text: YOU, MY FRIEND, ARE AN ENTREPRENEUR!

Week 1 & 2

Lecture: Review chapters about Entrepreneurship, Business Plan, Strategic Plan and 5-Year Budget.
Discussion: Questions and answers on topics
Research: Mentees will choose their industry and partner and begin working on their research papers in APA style.

The partners can split assignments as they desire. One can work on the research paper and the other on the business plan or something else. They may also choose to work together. Give them the option.

The research paper will be written in APA style placing the reference in the body of the paper. Example:

William Glasser, MD, in The Quality School (1989) states fun, safety and love should be included in the learning experience.

Week 3

Continue reviewing Chapters discussed in first two weeks. Also, discuss chapter about Communication Skills.

Discussion: Questions and answers about Communication Skills & any other previously taught topics.
Research: Mentees will continue to compile research paper, business plan, strategic plan & 5-year budget.

Week 4.

Lecture: Continue discussion about Communication Skills
Discussion: Question & answer period
Research: Mentees will continue compiling research paper, business plan, strategic plan, and 5-year budget.

Week 5.

Lecture: Chapter Principle of Accounting & Management
Discussion: Question & answer period
Research: Mentees will continue working on documents listed above
Months: April, July, October

Week 1.

Lecture: Getting Identification Number and Articles of Incorporation
Discussion: Questions & answers period
Research: Mentees will continue working on project documents.

Week 2.

Lecture: Continue discussion topics from Week 1.
Discussion: Question & answer period
Research: Mentees are continuing their work on project documents.

Week 3.

Lecture: Review the topics discussed from week 1 & 2. Also discuss Succession Planning.
Discussion: Questions & answer period

Week 4.

Lecture: Continue lecture about Communication Skills
Discussion: Question & answer period.
Research: Mentees will continue compiling their research papers.

Week 5.

Lecture: Continue discussing Principles of Accounting & Management
Discussion: Question & answer period
Research: Mentees will continue compiling their research papers.

EXTRA PROJECT

You may purchase separately a separate handbook entitled HANDBOOK FOR COLLEGE SCHOLARS from publisher.

If not, continue working on research paper and other documents getting ready for Business Fair.

CLASS AAA – ADVANCE

| MONTHS: MARCH, JUNE, SEPTEMBER

Motto: I SEE THE VISION, I'M MOTIVATED TO ACT, THE FUTURE IS UP TO ME.
Lecture: Intellectual Properties & Succession Planning

Week 1.

Lecture: Continue from initial discussion
Discussion: Questions & answers
Research: Mentees will choose a business industry and begin working on their research paper. Discuss criteria for paper, i.e. APA style etc.

Week 2.

Lecture: Succession Planning
Discussion: Questions and answers. Mentees will also submit their research topic. Additionally, introduce mentees to business plan, strategic plan and 5-year budget.
Research: Mentees will work on their research paper and business papers for Business Fair.

Week 3.

Lecture: Continue teaching about research and business papers.
Discussion: Question & answers.
Research: Mentees continue working on research paper and business paperwork.

Week 4.

Lecture: Principles of Accounting & Balance Sheet
Discussion: Questions and answer on lecture topics
Also, introduce the 5-year budget used in Excel
Research: Mentees continue their research and working on project topics using the business plan, strategic plan, 5-year budget
Months: April, July, October

FROM A HANDBOOK

Lecture: Investing Like the Wealthy in Tangible Assets

Week 1.

Lecture: from above topic
Discussion: Questions & answers
Research: Mentees finalize their research in preparation for Business Fair

Week 2.

Review any topic mentees desire
Discussion: Questions and answers from review
Research: Mentees will continue working on preparation for Business Fair.

Week 3.

Lecture: Discuss the Business Fair
Discussion: Questions & answers pertaining to Business Fair and any topic the mentees desire.
Everything should be near completion and final mounting of all information on three-sided board. Mentees will practice their presentations and explaining their board information.

Month: May, August, November
Lecture: Discuss one of the suggested books like THINK & GROW RICH, THE RICHEST MAN IN BABYLON ETC.
FOCUS ON PREPARATION FOR BUSINESS FAIR. ANNOUNCE THE DATE, TIME ETC.

BUSINESS FAIR

Mentees will present their final projects at the Business Fair. This will be an evening event for parents, friends etc. to attend. Business topics cannot include liquor stores, hair salons or Bar B Que restaurants. Mentees will purchase the following materials:

CLASS A – ELEMENTARY

1. Three-sided board
2. Lettering
3. Paper
4. Construction paper
5. Pencils & pens
6. Access to computer

CLASS AA – HIGH SCHOOL

1. Three-sided board
2. Lettering
3. Note paper
4. Construction paper
5. Pencils and pens
6. Access to computers

CLASS AAA – ADVANCE

1. Use of Power-point or handouts
2. Other materials as necessary
3. Access to computer

AWARD CERTIFICATES

BUSINESS FAIR BOARD MOUNTING
LEFT SIDE   CENTER   RIGHT SIDE

Vision Statement Abstract   5-year budget
Mission Statement   Business Plan
Strategic Plan

2-inch lettering across top of three-sided board

BUSINESS FAIR

The Business Fair should be held in a gymnasium, auditorium or another huge area to accommodate participates and visitors.

Prior to the Fair, notify the media and others to make them aware of the accomplishments of the mentees. Chances are, they have number seen a Business Fair and will find the experience very interest.

Prior to the Fair, allow mentees to meet with their partners and practice among themselves. You may want to observe and give input. Remember, do not allow them to read from papers but use the paper as a guide.

Also, encourage them to dress for success and wear their Sunday best on the day of the presentations. An hour or two prior to the Fair, have the mentees or facility staff to set up tables and chairs for the presenters and guest. Have a mentee give the Welcome! This is their day they should enjoy it.

It is imperative that the mentees learn TO WORK ON THE BUSINESS PRIOR TO WORKING IN THE BUSINESS!

ENJOY AND HAPPY SAILING!

ABOUT THE AUTHOR

Dr. Reginald T. Hardaway, Sr. was an educator and professor who taught in the graduate schools of Education & Business Administration for Olivet Nazarene University and Concordia University.

He holds a BS degree in Business Administration and Finance from the University of Arkansas at Pine Bluff, a MS degree in Hospital & Health Administration with an internship in hospital administration from the University of Cincinnati and a Ed. D in Education Leadership with a minor in the DBA program of Business Management from Sarasota University.

Dr. Hardaway has previously taught at Benedictine University, Rosary College, North Park University-Chicago, Chicago City Colleges & Chicago Public Schools.

Additionally, he has worked in healthcare for Bethesda Hospital in Cincinnati, Ohio and Cook County Hospital in Chicago. His corporate experience includes Sears Headquarters where he worked in Marketing and Buying Administration. He has also worked in broadcasting for Jana Broadcasting (WMPP 1470) and Chicago Broadcasting where he was an on-air personality and later Vice President of Finance at newly formed Chicago Broadcasting.

Dr. Hardaway's publications include: "The Keys to America's Kingdom: Economics, Education & Politics", An Historical Case Study of a Quality Classroom", The Formation, Organization of a Sickle Cell Center", An Alphabet Cuisine for Managers", "How You Can Become A Successful Entrepreneur", and a series of Handbooks.

He has received numerous awards and nominations including: "Who's Who in America's Education", Distinguished Leadership Award for Outstanding Contribution to Contemporary Society", Outstanding Young Man of America", and the Archbishop James P. Lyke African American Male Image Award".

Dr. Hardaway has also served as motivational and graduation speaker throughout Illinois and seminar presenter for the University of Illinois – Chicago.

Born in Chicago, Illinois, Dr. Hardaway is a product of great parents, a great church, Mt. Calvary BC, John D. Shoop Elementary School, and Morgan Park High School where he lettered in baseball and later played in Chicago's Comiskey Park and Municipal Stadium in West Palm Beach, Florida. He is a born again Christian and the father of two sons.